To David & Mary
with smiles &
grins!

Cullen R. Murphy

THE WAKING HOUR

A COLLECTION OF ILLUSTRATED VERSE

BY

CHARLES R. MURPHY

TRUE NORTH STUDIO

KANGAROO IN A ROCKER

Kangaroo in a rocker
Bright sunlight filling the room.
Draw the shade to make it darker
Stay in bed till after noon.

Sleeping in until its late
will assign a heavy cost.
You must get up on the run
And the morning will be lost.

ADRIFT

Four sheep and a goat
Set off in a boat
Across a deepening sky.

The houses below
Could not really know
One sheep was wondering "Why?"

"Forget this odd crew
meandering through
sky that is threatening storm."

"Its better I go
to join those below
whose homes seem friendly and warm."

So over the side
She leapt in a stride;
Left them to go on their way.

Observed from a hill
They're wandering still
Amongst clouds to this very day.

ORIGINAL

I had a thought I thought was mine.
I thought about it for some time.

Was I the only one who had
that novel thought or was I mad?

And then I came upon a lad
Who shared with me a thought he had.

It was the same one I had known
And here he thought it was his own!

We talked about the many more
Who might have had that thought before.

A common thought inside our head
That's never spoken, never said.

We cannot claim we had it first
For fear our bubble may be burst.

To own a thought exclusively
Cannot be proved decisively.

There is no proof that can attest
Save how you make thought manifest.

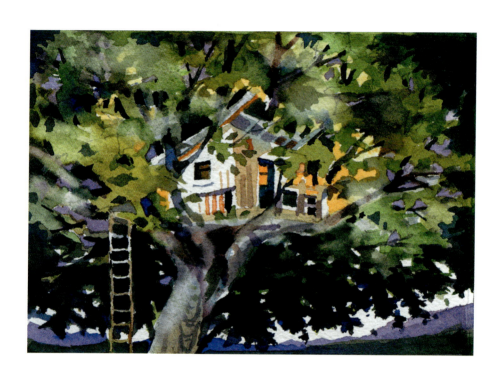

TREEHOUSE

Mickey built a treehouse
Of scavenged sticks and boards.

He climbed up on a ladder
Made of braided cords.

This place was his and his alone
So no one else came near.

He'd stay up there for hours
Without a care or fear.

It was great for make-believe
That no one else could see.

Hidden by the summer leaves
He acted out with glee.

While playing super-hero
Or reading comic books,

He never had to suffer
Disapproving looks.

When he came down he joined again
The world of ordinary.

He couldn't wait to climb back up
Where no one was contrary.

BAD DREAM

At night in dreams sometimes we see
A certain something dark that might
Reach out and grab us viciously
While we tremble clutched by fright.

But in the instant it gets near
We have the power to erase.
By waking up we chase the fear
Away to hide some other place.

BUG

I watched a bug crawl up to me
And pass on by unknowingly.

It made me wonder if he thought
That I was something I was not.

If he hadn't moved I wouldn't know
There was something live below.

Could something of his tiny size
Ever fully recognize

That I could step upon that spot
And make of him a little blot?

When next you gaze up in the skies
Think about such things as size.

For those above who fly with wings
See us below as tiny things.

CHANGE

There are some things that we do not know
But like to think that it isn't so.

But soon enough we find out quite fast
Our circumstances just do not last.

You should be alert for things that could change
Be well advised to then re-arrange;

Things that you thought were certainly true
Might really be false and turn upon you.

STUBBORN

Mr. Blue Jay is a pest.
He's picked a spot to build his nest,

Above the place I like to sit
And now he's made a mess of it.

I've chased him off a time or two
But he returns to build anew.

I'm sure that he will give up soon.
I'll stand on guard until its noon.

The two of us are stubborn though.
I'm betting that he'll have to go.

'Cause Mrs. Jay is staying near
and to her its very clear.

She will not wait, or ask, or beg
Its time for her to lay her egg.

So he must hurry, he must race
To build a nest some other place.

NIGHT

A bird in the flowers
Was counting the hours
Till dawn would bring him some light.

Until it was time
The moonlight would shine
and fairies would fly through the night.

Revealed in the glow
Were beings that know
That they could be seen in the day.

Its better to wait
Till after its late
So that they can frolic and play.

The bird stayed quite still
And watched them until
A glow appeared in the sky.

They noticed it too
And all but a few
Gave in and went fluttering by.

With all of them gone
He started his song
And greeted a promising day.

Soon others joined in
Creating a din
That drove any darkness away.

CHOCOLATE

Most of us like chocolate.
We have since we were young.
It has a unique flavor,
Its smooth upon your tongue.

On ice cream we like syrup.
In cookies we put chips.
Too much chocolate women say
Is worn upon their hips.

Folks like it in their coffee
Or in a piece of cake.
No matter where you put it
You'll want some more to take.

You can get it in a drizzle.
It comes in chunks and bars,
Or in some chocolate kisses
And even chocolate stars.

We shape it into bunnies
And many other things.
How it looks won't matter;
It's the pleasure that it brings.

We give it to our loved ones
To show them that we care.
No matter how we get it,
Its lots of fun to share.

BOAT

There once was a sailor named Chips
Who fancied the building of ships.
He planned his own boat
To spend time afloat
With good friends who laughed at his quips.

Intending to build her indoors
The drawings were done on the floors.
The plans that he made
Were never mislaid,
But had to be read on all fours.

He worked on his dream until late
Steering the course of her fate.
The ship grew so big
That Chips had to rig
A cradle that held all her weight.

The yacht was a source of his pride,
Something he just couldn't hide.
The problem he found
Was getting around
The fact that he'd built her inside.

Now how would he get the boat out?
A question that left him in doubt.
His good friends from town
helped take a wall down.
"She's free!" cried Chips with a shout.

FLIGHT

I rode astride a flitting sparrow
Who flew between the trees.
The passages were much too narrow.
"I think I'll dismount, if you please."

He perched on branch above a stream
And I got off to look.
He left me stranded in the dream.
"Now, how to reach the brook?"

To climb to earth became my quest.
I picked my way with care.
My heart was pounding in my chest.
Swallows flew in from the air.

"We'll take you to the nearer shore,"
They said assuredly.
They swooped in arcs but gently bore
Me down below the tree.

Flying high above the blue
Becomes a wishful thought;
Enjoying what a bird can do
That human folk cannot.

INSPIRED

Where do great ideas start?
In the brain or in the heart?

A canvas with no image there
Suggests too much when it is bare.

You have to wonder what could be
When first you look but do not see.

An image forms from where you feel,
Now its your task to make it real.

So let it out, express yourself;
Don't keep it bottled on the shelf.

Inspiration comes to all
But not all artists heed its call.

Some let it pass without concern,
Confident it will return.

But they lament when its not there
If only they had paused to care.

STARS

Place the moon where the sun would be
And stars come out immediately.

All along they've been right there
Just hidden in the sunny glare.

When we send ourselves to sleep
We ask that God, the stars will keep,

And tomorrow when we rise
We'll be stars in someone's eyes.

END

Kangaroo in a rocker.
Young monkey up in a tree.
These animals couldn't care less
About what happens to me.

Oh, but I should be watching
The final fate that befalls
Creatures out there unlike us
That never live within walls.

The last of their earthly days
Should surely make me aware
Of the damaging things we are doing
Without a regard or a care.

In noting what happens to them
I should be able to see
A semblance of some kind of end
That could be in store for me.

Be a very good steward
Wherever it is you are,
Practicing kindness toward nature
Both near and also afar.

© 2010 Charles R. Murphy

All rights reserved. No part of this book may be reproduced or transmitted in any form or by any means, electronic or mechanical, including photocopying, recording, or by any information storage and retrieval system, without permission in writing from the publisher.

Published by True North Studio
518 W. 8th Street, Traverse City, Michigan 49684
www.artistsnorth.com/murphy

Publisher's Cataloging-in-Publication Data
Murphy, Charles R.

    The waking hour : a collection of illustrated verse / Charles R. Murphy.
    – Traverse City, Mich. : True North Studio, 2010.

    p. ; cm.

    Summary: A collection of rhyming verse written and illustrated in watercolor by Michigan artist Charles R. Murphy.

    ISBN13: 978-0-9845798-0-8

    I. Title.
    PS3613.U77 2010
    813.6—dc22

Cover and interior design by ion design

Printed in the United States of America
14 13 12 11 10 • 5 4 3 2 1